Praise for *Poems for a World on Fire*

Poems for a World on Fire is the perfect nam~ ^
of poems, poems which speak of cour~
hope. Helen's artistry, her words, are .
to read and understand yet profound ε
for her personal struggles and our collec   ~u
earth's suffering. Her poems are filled witl   ₊apital T),
some of it hard-hitting, some comforting. I wish we could
have had this collection as a guide from the first COVID-19
diagnosis, from the first California fire. But we have them
now, and can all be led to more skillful action and deeper hope.

—Susan Lebel Young, author of
*Food Fix: Ancient Nourishment for Modern Hunger*s
and *Lessons from a Golfer: A Daughter's Story of Opening the Heart*

Helen's words are stepping-stones on a journey of realism
where she brings us from comfort to questioning, to
acknowledging and claiming gratitude for what is before
us. The emotional visionary signposts which she explores
in these poems are something we all have known and
experienced. Her words sear with the fire of transformation,
while offering a personal invitation to ultimately feel the
ever-changing and awakening dance of life.

—Marsie Silvestro, poet and author of
Feast of Sisterly Trance Formation,
Grief Walks Through Me Like a Rake,
and *The Sky Is My Ocean*

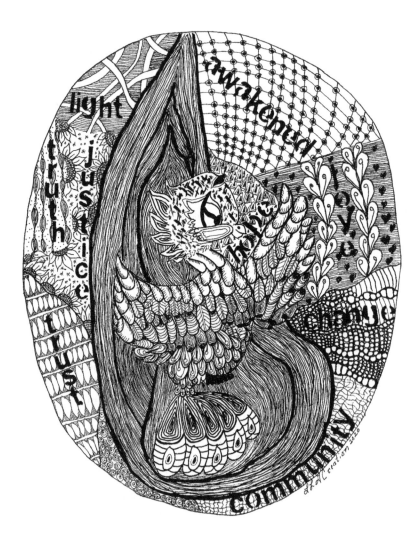

Poems for a World on Fire

Meditations on Hope

Helen G. Rousseau

Poems for a World on Fire
© 2020 Helen G. Rousseau
ISBN 978-1-7361116-0-4

Cover photo-illustration and cover and book design by Lindy Gifford
Frontispiece illustration by Laura Carey
Genie Dailey, editor

Rousseau Publishing
www.helenrousseau.com

With gratitude
for all who work toward a healthier planet

and

for those first responders and health care workers
who ignore the buzz of politics
and do an outstanding job,
day after day,
taking their lives into their hands
serving COVID-19 patients.

Foreword

"But it isn't easy," said Pooh to himself, as he looked at what had once been Owl's House. "Because Poetry and Hums aren't things which you get, they're things which get you. And all you can do is to go where they can find you."

—A. A. Milne, *The House at Pooh Corner*

When I first began gathering poems for this collection, I was already overwhelmed with the challenges we are facing in this century: never-ending wars, refugee camps, hunger, racism, ageism, domestic violence, increasing poverty, global warming, deforestation, and loss of animal habitat. Then the novel coronavirus burst on the scene and life as we knew it changed drastically as our world was turned upside down. The title, *Poems for a World on Fire*, came to me in 2019, before we began experiencing the devastating wildfires out west in 2020.

Considering all this, we seek comfort, find places that renew us, like the ocean, lakes, or labyrinth walks. Phone calls with friends are more important than ever.

Reading the daily posts on social media, writing poems to express my feelings at this time, and receiving poems from friends experiencing negative or positive aspects of quarantine, I realized that sharing our emotions helped us to face these trials knowing we are not alone. May your reading of these poems make you feel less alone and maybe inspire you to write your own feelings in poetry or prose.

Have a journal ready to write your reactions. Use the title of the poem as a prompt for your own writing. Share your thoughts with friends. Writing is such a good tool to help us navigate our emotions and responses to what's happening in the world around us.

I chose a yin–yang symbol for the cover to remind us that balance in all things is what we are striving for. These poems are my attempt to focus on the good around us from first responders, the beauty of nature, the love of family and friends, and our own inner beauty and courage as we face those challenges that sometimes feel overwhelming.

Thank you for walking this path with me.
Helen G. Rousseau

Contents

Introduction

Sometimes when I travel on roads covered with asphalt, I can almost hear the ground below it crying to me: "My breath fails me, my voice is silenced by noises overhead. My land is barren for lack of sun and rain. I once was rich and beautiful with grasses, flowers, and trees, but progress has meant covering these lands, free for millions of years. This does not stop me from springing up whenever I sense a crack in the roads or sidewalks. I seek the fresh air and the warmth of the sun, and I endure."

Mother Earth also cries out for all the oppressed over the centuries. She cries out for women who are one with her as nurturers, life-givers, whose gifts have been taken for granted, and who have been raped by greed and destruction as she has. She cries out for men to balance the energy that they have usurped for themselves and have tipped the power in only one direction.

Mother Earth is always a teacher if we will listen. She gave us the seasons to remind us that life is cyclical, each season with its own gifts and beauty, teaching patience and the gift of waiting. She gives us the lightning storms, earthquakes, monsoons, and hurricanes so we can see destruction and not want to replicate it in our lives with bombs and wars. She is the Mother protected by Father Sky, and they desperately need each other in balance to survive. Father Sky needs his ozone layer to continue protecting us from the destructive rays of the sun.

Humans have come to believe that they can control the gifts the Mother generously bestows. As if her corn is not good enough, we must modify it genetically. Her rivers don't suit our needs, so we dam them up. Her seasonal fruits and vegetables are limited, so we must cart them in from other countries, disregarding whether they are safe to eat or not. Her great rainbow color of peoples hasn't taught us acceptance as she thought it would but has transformed fear of others into hatred and prejudice and even war.

As a mother with an unruly child, she has been patient and sent us warning prophets to call us back to her loving heart, but our ears have been closed because we thought we knew better. Now she is sending other prophets who are crying loudly against the destruction humans have created. The future will be decided by those who will listen and act for the common good.

These are the feelings of my heart, the inspiration for this poetry, which is my attempt to be a voice for the earth, its peoples, animals, trees, seas, land, and all that makes this planet uniquely our home.

Courage

A Place of Comfort

Bottom of the well empty,
I stood before the wild mother,
breathed in her holy sea breath
as breezes caressed my lost soul.

I was home again,
hungry, thirsty, seeking
comfort not available
for too many years.

Every spare moment
found me there
lost in her embrace,
resurrecting feelings long dormant.

She was always waiting,
welcoming my arrival
with salty kisses
and gentle enfoldment.

Day after day, I let her
energize me,
fill me with courage.
Now, wherever I am,

she is within me,
my soul renewed,
trusting all is well in
the ebb and flow of my life.

Trust

In fear, I contract, fold in
on myself, creating barriers
I presume will make me safe.

Keeping at bay what scares me,
I forget that an embrace
of fear releases its bindings.

Like a butterfly,
I work to uncoil from the cocoon
which protected my fragility.

With trust, I expand,
arise from the silence within,
move forward to spread my wings,

trusting I will be held aloft
by life, where the winds of change
challenge me in new directions.

Creativity's Birth

Barren womb
cries to my soul
in these later years of life:
*You forget me at
your own peril.*

Post-menopausal body
that never birthed children or
nursed them to life,
wastes no time weeping
for what it never had
nor mourning what was lost.

This womb's life is not over,
though withered in its tomb,
nor is mine,
now shriveled in its skin,
outer layer simply
a comfortable shell.

New surge of longing
whispers from opened heart:
*You are fertile and moist,
seed-ready and able to bring
forth new creations from
nothing but desire.*

Living Alone

Living alone as one ages—
a paradox—walking the path
cautiously between
solitude and loneliness.

Being alone in a pandemic
can be a blessing. More time
to meditate, read, refocus
on the soul's journey.

Sometimes, it can feel like
a jail sentence, a forced enclosure
testing the limits of
patience and endurance.

I've experienced both
at one time or another.
Solitude—a path to wonder,
loneliness—a heart longing for more.

No family to worry about.
No family to share with.
No partner to annoy me.
No partner to support me.

A tightrope walk,
keeping the balance between
letting go to despair
or finding joy in the journey.

Creative Solitude

With few distractions and no commitments
during this time of social distancing,
I am challenged by my solitude.
It calls me to live deeply
with an inner strength I didn't know I had.

Ordered to stay inside to stop the spread
of a virus that challenges
the best medical minds,
every decision I make to live safely
is a gift to myself and others.

In this quiet space, I access
the creativity that becomes
my partner in isolation.
I accept the opportunity this presents,
aware of how lucky I am.

When the cocoon becomes too confining,
a butterfly emerges.
When the rain stops and the sun appears
from behind the clouds,
a rainbow is painted across the sky.

When death becomes a daily event,
life feels more precious than ever.

I Stand in My Space

I stand in my space
not hunched in fear
or anxiety. My center
of balance strong, not rigid.

What was once glazed over—
smoke screens preventing clarity—
has cleared in the face
of truth spoken boldly.

The demons that drained
my sense of self
have perished in their streams
of broken promises.

My inner core has become
so strong that the winds of
change befriend me
and carry me as I fly.

The Phoenix

"Don't be afraid of the ashes,"
said the Phoenix.
"It may feel like everything
is dying, slowly turning
to what you fear
may be the end of the journey.

My new wings are here
to tell you:
Rise!
It is just the beginning,
black turning to green.
No death here, never death,
only change
and transformation."

One Swift Stroke

"If you don't like it,
you can walk," you tell me,
as if it was as easy as
opening the door
and leaving behind a life
that we have built from
our loneliness and dreams,
leaving the only home I've known,
the only partner I've had
and supported unconditionally.
As if I can walk anywhere
when you stand in the doorway
and don't let me pass,
take my keys or glasses
so I can't drive away.
You tell me to walk as if
there is no cord that binds us
to each other, which I
finally must cut with
one swift stroke
and not look back.

This Perfect Summer Day

It is the end of a perfect summer day,
a day of gentle breezes through my windows,
pickling cucumbers from my garden,
and snuggling with my cat, who keeps me
living in the present moment.
I decide to end my day at the beach,
uniting my rhythm with the eternal waves.

It is less crowded than usual
since tourists are limited in coming here.
I relish the ocean smells, the gulls' screeches,
the children playing, the people swimming.
Not far away at the local hospital,
and at hospitals around the world,
doctors, nurses, and other staff
are doing all they can to keep people alive.

Such a contrast is not lost on me
as I share my journey with two friends
challenged with illnesses
determined to bring them down.
But they know, as I do,
that in every moment there is a choice
of how we will respond.

Listening to the Goddess Within

Before you need to call me,
I'll be listening.
I've always been listening,
but the priests did not speak for you.
Nor did they listen to me as
I cried in the wilderness
of my church.
The world did not speak for you, either.
I wandered in its byways
trying to make my home there.

I remember the first time you called me,
filled my heart with wonder.
I remember when you ceased to call,
or maybe I wasn't listening then,
overwhelmed by a betrayal of love.
I never found you there, either.

Alone once again, I sought you
in the vastness and power of the sea.
The tides spoke your name.
I sought you in the earth.
I called you Mother.
The flowers showed me your face.
I sought you in the eyes of friends.
You looked at me with love.

The Masses Have Awakened

The days of the prophets
are past, long gone
into the annals of history.
The fear of the Lord no longer
a tool to keep the masses in check.

Some keep trying to resurrect
the old ways of control
in the name of an unseen God,
to further their own purposes
and unfounded beliefs.

But the masses have awakened
to the truth of human connection:
We all survive together
or perish from the idolatry
of money and power.

A Daughter's Lament

No amount of reasoning,
compassion, and understanding
of my mother's life
could stop tears from flowing
as I visited her once again.
"Don't cry," was all she could say,
as the pain of what never was
engulfed me to paralysis.

I couldn't speak the words
lodged in my throat,
squeezing my heart
of any hope it had left
for receiving the comfort
it had longed for
since its first days
of awareness in the crib.

Both of us at peace now,
I know that what I needed then
was beyond her ability to give.
I choose to remember her actions
that spoke of a mother's
devotion to the role she embraced
with all she had to give.

Learning to Make Fire

From the beginning
in covens of old
to the women uniting today,
we seek new ways
for our spirits to rise.

As women at the edges
of a patriarchy
that is slowly dying,
as women at the forefront
of justice for all,
we are creating a new fire
to burn the texts that have
given men domination,
to burn all the words
that demean,
to burn all ideas that have
led to intolerance.

We are creating a fire
of truth and love
to light the way
for a new generation.

Challenges

Fear Will Not Lead Us

Fear will not lead us
out of the swamp,
over the mountain,
or through the fire.

Lies will not give us
the map to our future
or make us more loving
to one another.

Only truth-telling informs us
of paths to be taken,
challenges to overcome,
and possibilities to embrace.

Only love can unite us
as brothers and sisters
in the goal of our
planet's salvation.

A World on Fire

War in the name of a cause,
a god, or a perceived truth
is a travesty of the humanity
that calls us as brothers and sisters
to a world community.

We are the saviors the world
is waiting for. We are the ones
who are called to act,
speak up, join hands
across perceived barriers,

and work to prevent the useless
destruction of forests, homes,
and natural habitat, in the name
of causes that have lost
their relevance in a world on fire.

Meditation on Grieving

I take in deep breaths of hope
and release deep breaths of despair
as I grieve the loss of civility,
the rampant disregard for truth.

I take in deep breaths of faith
and release deep breaths of doubt
as I grieve the use of religion
to lead many astray from truth.

I take in deep breaths of love
and release deep breaths of hate
as I grieve the loss of leadership
from those who use power to sow division.

Somewhere in this universe,
faith, hope, and love still abide.
I breathe in these qualities
that they may come and dwell in me.

Six Feet Apart

No hugs hello or goodbye,
only caution as we place
our chairs six feet apart.

Seven months since this virus
began and moved steadily
around the world.

Five months since we heard
the command to quarantine,
wash hands, wear a mask.

A "flu" that was supposed
to disappear attacked with fury
instead, not giving up control.

Weary of being careful,
we want to break out of detention,
but the daily numbers keep us home.

In my solitude, I ponder the grace
of each moment, the time to be
present to myself unconditionally.

It is a time for patience and courage,
to renew commitments to hope
in the present and for the future.

No Battle Plan

We know we are at war.
With no unified battle plan,
the death count rises.
Fifty states with fifty different
ideas how this should be handled.
Its citizens at the mercy
of politics which present
no reasonable plan at all.

How long will the people
wait until their lives
become more important
than the ideologies of their leaders?
How long must they suffer
the loss of loved ones
who die alone
and in immense pain?

The beloved community
is shattered…or was it ever
there at all?

These Masks

If only it were Halloween
and we were donning these masks
to beg for candy or attend a party
where food and drink flow easily.

A temporary protection,
it has become a barrier
between health and a plague,
between believers and naysayers.

There is no competition
for prettiest or ugliest,
as we focus only on safety,
mine and yours.

Reading George Orwell
did not prepare me for the reality
now before me, a more frightening
enemy that could take my life.

It's hard to believe that in
this century of science and physics,
some still deny what is seen
with their eyes.

Yes, the earth is round, a man
did walk on the moon, a space station
is circling our planet, and a virus
is more contagious than any we've ever seen.

In Time

In time, this thing I call life
will be no more.
Time itself, an illusion
we try to make real
with clocks and calendars:
all arbitrary and limiting.

Indigenous peoples
synchronized their lives
with Mother Earth,
observing the cycles of the moon,
planting and harvesting
in tune with the seasons.

The so-called civilized
needed to control time
as they needed to control
everything else, as well as each other.
This, the true fall from grace,
that in time we will understand.

Returning to Balance

Mother Earth's heartbeat,
heard in the ebb and flow
of the ocean, speaks to us
of a failure to honor her gifts,
her family of animals
losing habitat,
rain forests destroyed
for farming, feeding the
hunger for beef.
Coral reefs are dying
because of human
interference that continues
to warm up our only home.

I pray that her heart
continues to beat
with hope as she waits
for humanity to finally
realize what she has
always known:
The laws of nature
are sacred,
must be honored,
or suffer the consequences.

Only humility will return
us to balance.

Sometimes

Sometimes,
many times,
I kneel beside my bed and pray.
Sometimes, many times,
that is all I can do.

When an animal becomes extinct,
a child is abandoned,
or someone dies trying
to reach a place of freedom,
I kneel beside my bed and pray.

I do not pray to anyone.
I only allow my soul to cry out
with the pain of the world
as I reach deep within
for what my answer will be.

Do I change anything this way?
I don't know,
but I believe
compassion is the
beginning of action.

The Grief of the Earth

The grief of the earth
rises through our bodies,
spills out through our eyes.
She no longer can tolerate
the destruction
of her glorious body,
her rivers and streams,
her animals and plants,
and of us, her beloveds.

We have seen the decline
in animal species and habitat,
pollution of water and air,
the migration of millions
seeking a better way to live,
and yet we persist in our ways.

She sent a sixteen-year-old prophet
who didn't mince her words,
who was listened to by the masses
but not by the leaders.
And here we are today,
in a trial by fire,
a pandemic loosed upon the earth.

She now has our attention,
begging us to act while there is still time.
Will we finally listen?

The Wages of Sin

While politicians take their bribes,
unashamedly called donations,
from powerful lobbies,
our children go to school,
look around their classrooms,
and wonder which student
might be capable of pulling
a gun on them someday.

While taxes are lowered
on the rich to promote
business with lies of a
trickle-down effect to everyone,
the masses line up in food pantries,
colleges provide food and clothing
to students, and parents work
three jobs to make ends meet.

The animals and plants
that have become extinct
cannot shame us to conversion.
The earth Mother,
who is losing her children,
continues to cry out to us,
through the quickly changing climate,
that her patience is at an end.

My Life Mattered

I know what it's like
to feel your life doesn't matter.
So long ago, but I remember.
Warts on hands
I hid under the desk
when the nun came by.

A friend's mother,
looking at my dirty kid self,
assessing if she wants
her daughter to play with
this scruffy girl
who knows that look.

Roller skating with a friend
who comments on the bugs
crawling on my neck.
I run home to where
another round of foul-smelling
liquid gets poured on my hair.

Neglect was what I knew
as a child. Teeth covered with tartar,
my hand would hide my smile.
For years, my outward appearance
humbled me. I feared someone
would discover the truth.

However,

I never, ever, was pulled
over because I was white.
My car was never searched
for drugs. My home never
broken into, a gun
pointed at my head.

I have received kindness
and deference because I was a nun.
Officers have smiled, given me
warnings because of my white hair.
My skin color never put fear
into a shop clerk.
My presence never made
anyone step aside,
wondering if I would hurt them.
Though I wasn't aware of it,
I walked with white privilege,
expecting proper behavior
toward me at all times.

I have prided myself
in not taking life for granted,
always grateful for what I have.
I never realized, until now,
the protections that my
white skin provides me.

Puzzles

Halfway through putting together
this puzzle, I am looking for all
the blue pieces, this particular color blue.

With the puzzle pieces spread out,
I scan carefully across the table,
find two more and place them where
they belong. I am sure

I have looked with an eagle eye,
yet two blue pieces are still missing.
Is it this way with life, when certainty
keeps at bay what is right before our eyes?

Longing

Deep within each earthly being,
a poignant cry begins.

Rising from unmet need,
it seeks kindred spirits.

A unified voice begins the chant
of want and need and longing.

The power of this chorus
shatters the walls

no one
thought could fall.

Hope

A Paradox

Hummingbirds sip the nectar
from the feeder provided them.
Squirrels run to and fro,
chasing each other
and raiding the bird feeders.
Rory, my black cat, sleeps
in the sun knowing only comfort.

Hospitals are overburdened.
Loved ones die alone.
Fear, a great motivator
for wearing masks and
social distancing.
Yet some choose self
over the greater good.

Let safety begin with me,
love guide my every choice,
as I keep moving with hope
toward a better future.
This I believe: We are one
community that will survive
or perish together.

It Doesn't Matter

To reach contentment,
allow my soul its needed respite,
I face the winds of confusion,
all that calls me out of balance,
the wildfire thoughts
that defy control,
and from my inner being
I say with all my knowing:
It doesn't matter.

The truth flows
from the river of grace
that nourishes all in its path:
the barren ground,
the wounded soul,
the roots of trees,
and the underpinnings of hope.

What matters is this one thing:
I am alive!

Walking the Labyrinth

I leave my cares at the entry
to this inviting labyrinth
built with stones, hope,
and a deep intention for renewal.

My feet, not used to walking slowly,
must be told to take their time—
the goal to experience
fully the journey I've begun.

I walk a circular path, but I'm
not going around in circles.
Unlike a maze, the way is clear,
carefully marked.

I come into the center. I breathe,
slowly letting go of things
that no longer serve me, no longer
bring me joy and peace.

I leave a shell to represent this walk,
to show I was here with intention.
I walk back the way I came,
with lighter heart and renewed purpose.

We Are All One

Whether you walk in a church,
genuflect and cross yourself,
or put on your tefillin, binding
your heart to the God of your fathers,
whether you raise your arms
as you sway to Gospel music
or kneel and bow to Allah
as you recommit yourself
to live by God's holy word,

whether you dance around a fire
to honor the Great Mother,
or walk the beach and sense
a moment of transcendence,
the Creator of the ever-expanding
universe, of the indisputable
laws of nature, responds:
"Do you know we are all one
in the heart of love?"

Enough

It is enough,
sitting in the car
facing the ocean—
glistening water, billowing waves—
long walks denied
by muscles in spasm.

It is enough,
to receive this day—
each precious minute—
ignore chatter of mind,
explore deeper layers,
find jewels beneath.

It is enough,
to see, hear, feel—
allow life to be as it is—
to say with the Spirit
that moves over the waters:
"It is good!"

Haiku on a Winter's Day

Hiding behind clouds
No sun pierces the clear pane
Winter's cold returns

Curled in a fur ball
My cat rests in unknowing
I learn from her truth

Listening to the wind
I hear a new melody
Loneliness is gone

One's resting place lost
A mind in constant motion
Time travels too fast

White birches bending
Moving with grace in the breeze
My soul finds its way

On the wings of hope
My soul lives through each season
The circle of life

A Safe Haven

Wednesday is craft night.
We rotate from home to home,
bring a project to work on,
knitting, crocheting, or mending.
Telling stories is essential.
Sharing family joys and sorrows
binds us in this group experience.

Tonight, we meet on Zoom again,
wondering if we'll ever meet face to face.
Our conversation is lively, as usual,
but now more focused on how
we are surviving or thriving
in these days of lock-down
which we all agree are necessary.

Conversation never falters.
So much to share—children,
grandchildren, and for one of us,
great-grandchildren. This group
of women is a safe haven
for our emotions
and the hope of a new day.

A Mary Oliver Walk

I'm taking a Mary Oliver walk
this splendid September morning.
Only the usual animals
in this neighborhood,
squirrels and chipmunks,
but they give me pause,
bring me the awareness of
how all beings fight for their lives,
even the spider I took from the tub
with a piece of cardboard
and gently laid outside.

The neighbor's gardens delight
me as I try to identify the many
different flowers blooming there,
sweetly placed near the sidewalk
for passersby to admire.
For these few minutes,
I can drink in beauty in the life around me,
thank the flowers for their colors
and shapes, speak to the strong trees,
thank them for their shade.

All this is part of the whole of life,
even the trees burning in California,
the animals displaced or dying
from forest fires out of control.
The yin and yang of existence
on this earth, what has always been
and always will be as we move
slowly but steadily to a gentler,
more conscious approach to
life and each other.

The Morning Glories

Sitting with morning glories
in my garden
as before an altar of hope,
a sacred moment.

I've planted morning glories
wherever I've lived in Maine.
Being with them,
I experience a holy calm.

They look at me
and seem to say:
"All is right in the world, Helen,
all is right in the world.

Right here, right now,
this moment when you
are totally present,
nothing else matters.

The world around you can be
rotating in a vortex
that is self-defeating.
Let it do that.

Just be here. Absorb
the beauty we offer you,
the peace and wholeness you feel
whenever you sit with us.

And don't forget us when
the season is over.
Remember what happens
when we are together.

Remember. Trust that
next summer we will
meet again, in this garden
where hope begins."

The Robin

She didn't move as I walked by,
so I stopped and spoke to her.
"You are so beautiful," I said.
She spread her wings but didn't fly away.
Maybe she's caught in the brambles, I thought.
So I asked her.
I watched as she jumped from branch to branch
to let me know she was all right.
She looked very pregnant with new life,
just as I had been before I delivered
the book that is now alive on its own.

She flew up to another branch
and began singing. I was close enough
to see her beak move with song.
I thanked her for singing,
and she sang some more.
Back and forth we went with thank you
and song. With a full heart, I walked away
as she flew to secret places where
her song is cherished by the earth
and, for a moment in time, by me.

Haiku During a Pandemic

Dancing in the dark
I've yet to find my way
yet I dance on

I miss gentle touch
of friends who must stay distant
I long for reunion

Enjoying solitude
is freedom when it's chosen
not so today

Gazing out my window
daffodils teach a lesson
bloom where you're planted

Memories of the past
no longer haunt me
now that I know

When You Remember Me

When you remember me,
it will not be important
to say I was a nun,
that I wrote poetry
and songs
in my struggle to find my voice.

When you remember me,
I hope you can say
I was a faithful friend
with a compassionate heart.
Say how I loved my cats,
that making puzzles grounded me
and reading memoirs inspired me.

What I really hope you say is:
"She lived with integrity."

On This Beach

Let me die on this beach,
low tide, easy walking,
sun still warming my face
on this first September day.

Let me forever hear
the lapping of the waves,
music in my ears like
none other, calling me
to stay here and rest,

return to my original home.
No loneliness
or sense of loss
as I feel the embrace
of the tides, salt air,

as I breathe free and release
all that does not bring
me peace,
changing fear to trust,
holding on to letting go.

I want to rise like that kite…
and fly.

Acknowledgments

I want to express my gratitude to all those who have supported me on my life's journey and who have encouraged my writing. I call you my cheerleaders. There are too many to list here, but know that I appreciate all the kind words, the listening ears, your belief in me as a friend, mentor, soul sister, and writer.

Thank you to all the people who have attended my writing groups. It is an enormous joy to help someone find their voice through writing.

To the Creativity Circle—Heather Bruhl, Hilary Zayed, Kerry Kenney, and Mary Carol Kennedy—for providing a safe space to explore, share books, insights, joys, and trials as we support each other's artistic expression. To Elizabeth Gilbert's *Big Magic*, which guided our discussions and gave us the courage to express our own genius through whatever form of art we chose. We are painters, writers, weavers, musicians, and authors.

To Arthur Lavoie and Susan Findlay for teaching me about friendship, and to Patricia Spiller for teaching me about curiosity.

To Laura Carey for her beautiful Zentangle, a meditation on the themes in this book.

To Lindy Gifford of Manifest Identity, who knows how to do magic with a manuscript, and who also knows how to listen and help birth a project that first begins with a dream.

A special thanks to the one who provided me with the financial assistance to make this book a reality. I'm forever grateful.

About the Author

Writing poetry has been a constant in Helen's life. It is where she first found a voice. Eventually, her poems became songs, and she published three albums. She has also written essays and reflections, always finding inspiration in the world around her and in the simplest things, like hummingbirds at the feeder.

Poems for a World on Fire: Meditations on Hope is her third poetry book. *Early Childhood Education* was about her family and her attempt to make sense of her childhood. It was a very healing process. *Coming to the Edge: Fifty Poems for Writing and Healing* were the poems she wrote after leaving an abusive relationship. This book, with writing prompts, is a wonderful tool in writing groups as well as when one works solo or with a therapist. Helen has found, through the sharing of these poems, that we all, in some way, experience similar joys, struggles, transformative moments, and deep sorrow. It is always a comfort to know we are not alone.

Helen has her bachelor's and master's degrees in Theological Studies. She was a nun for thirty years and is now an ordained Interfaith Minister. (That journey is a story for another time.) She is a trained spiritual director to help people's faith journeys, no matter their beliefs. She also is certified in the Amherst Writers and Artists method to lead writing groups. Her hobby is carving block prints and designing tea towels. She can be reached at www.helenrousseau.com.

Also by Helen Rousseau
Coming to the Edge: Fifty Poems for Writing and Healing

In *Coming to the Edge,* readers are encouraged to engage with each of Helen's poems in ways that open up discoveries in their own lives. Prompts for reflection and writing accompany them, as well as affirmations for daily practice. This book is a great source for writing groups and for individual practice.

Praise for *Coming to the Edge*

Coming to the Edge is an inspirational compilation of beautifully written poems that help the reader to work through and heal from their painful places. The author's eloquent poetic reflections are an amazing gift to anyone who is on a spiritual or transforming journey of healing and recovery from painful life struggles. This book is a wonderful adjunct to psychotherapy, or as a tool for self-reflection to more deeply explore your inner world as you move toward personal growth and change. I highly recommend this book to all!

—Linda J. Cooke LICSW, LCSH, BCD

I discovered Helen, the book, the poetry, the insight she brings to her work two years ago. And what a discovery. Her writing is real, it's authentic, it comes from lived experience with layer upon layer of meaning and insight. Each time I pick it up I find something new, something I'd not seen before, something meaningful for that day.

—Pat Spiller, Master's Public Administration, Brandeis
Author, and fiber artist from Maine

The author takes you through an emotional, heartfelt journey that is so powerful that you are able to respond through your own life experiences. Each new page evokes emotions and takes you deeper into your thoughts and feelings, waking you up through eternal joy as you finish the book. One of those books that you can never really finish—you are always growing. Kudos to you, Helen, for helping me awaken my soul.

—Jodie Sands Dahl, Bachelor of Music
Certified peer specialist and survivor. Brainerd, Minnesota

Made in the USA
Middletown, DE
18 December 2020

28153667R00040